Out of Pain Came Poetry

Out of Pain Came Poetry

Tapping into the Greatness Within

Rev. Dr. Valerie Martin-Stewart

iUniverse, Inc.

New York Lincoln Shanghai

Out of Pain Came Poetry
Tapping into the Greatness Within

iUniverse books may be ordered through booksellers or by contacting:

iUniverse
2021 Pine Lake Road, Suite 100
Lincoln, NE 68512
www.iuniverse.com
1-800-Authors (1-800-288-4677)

ISBN-13: 978-0-595-39376-3 (pbk)
ISBN-13: 978-0-595-83774-8 (ebk)
ISBN-10: 0-595-39376-4 (pbk)
ISBN-10: 0-595-83774-3 (ebk)

Printed in the United States of America

Contents

PREFACE

The spiritual poetry and writings compiled in this book are expressions from deep within my heart over a 20-year span. Much of my writings express emotions that I was dealing with from as early as 4 years old, but was not able to adequately express those feelings and put them on paper until I was between 12-13 years old. Other of my writings were inspired by observing people that I have met along the way and felt some of what they were feeling. Sometimes the feelings were happy; sometimes they were sad; and sometimes they were an expression of just being tired, broken, and disgusted with living and the day-to-day challenges life would bring.

I found writing to be a great form of "release" when the pain within was too unbearable to utter aloud in words. I've always been made fun of when I was young. People laughed at the way I talked and walked. My heart has forever cried out longing to be loved and accepted, so I learned silence at a very young age and it soon became my best companion. However, when the silence became too much for me to bear, I prayed; crying out to the Lord God on high. And He taught me how to seek and get release and that release came through my writing.

There was a calling to preach on my life that I was battling and struggling with to receive and accept starting in the 11th grade. However, because of tradition, yes, that women are not called to preach but to be missionaries only, I ran and ran and ran. But the calling grew bigger in me day by week and month by year until I couldn't run any longer. So, you will find many of my writings and poetry expressing my desire to be "free." And that "freedom" <u>did</u> come on the day that I accepted my calling to preach. I discovered through that experience that even though I had never been physically locked behind prison bars, I was a prisoner at "another degree" as I tell in one of my poems. I believe many Christians as well as non-believers go where they want to go, do what they want to do, giving the appearance of freedom, but inwardly are deeply in bondage. They are all "locked up on the inside." Not able to express their hurt, addictions, rejection, pain, loneliness, silent frustrations and brokenness in a <u>positive</u> manner.

As you open this book of poems and writings and journey into my heart, I pray that you too will find healing for your soul and mind. For it is through and by way of the heart that we hear and understand ourselves, our God and the people around us. I simply live by an old saying of Shakespeare, "Be true to thy own self."

"So, journey with me if you dare
and find yourself and your release there"

Colossians 3:23 (KJV)
"And whatsoever ye do, do it heartily as to the Lord and not unto men"

ACKNOWLEDGMENTS

I honor and give thanks to my Lord and Savior Jesus Christ who saved me at the age of 8 years old and has never left me alone since. I thank His Holy Spirit for revealing unto me back in 1990 that my writing is a "gift" from God and it's not to be taken lightly. Therefore, it's not a choice any longer of mine of whether I will publish my material, for He's the giver of the gifts and the gifts are for "His" people.

I would also like to give thanks to my loving daughter, Paris Marie, who has encouraged me, listened to me read my poetry, and have been patient with me throughout this new endeavor.

To my dear pastor, friend, mentor, and confidante Pastor Endia J. Scruggs, I thank God for bringing you into my life and being a STABLE role model in and out of seasons.

I thank God for my dear sister Joyce who suggested adding scriptures with each poem & writing and it truly added volumes to this book.

I thank God for Shelly Williams who is responsible for taking photos "at the last minute" & for my dear friend, Rev. Elaine Rice who made it all possible.

I truly thank all my family, friends, teachers, pastors, and coaches who've made "deposits" into my life and spirit. And to all of you, those in the U.S. and Australia, who wrote me letters, notes, and spoke into my spirit over the years telling me that I needed to consider publishing my work for others to be blessed by it.

I want to thank my dear friend, Sharon Price-McEwen for being a voice of strength and wisdom during some of my most difficult days. I love you girl!

Psalms 119:71
"It is good for me that I have been afflicted that I might learn they statues"

"WE CAN WIN"

"Wherefore seeing we also are compassed about with so great a cloud of witnesses, let us lay aside every weight, and the sin which doth so easily beset us and let us run with patience the race that is set before us."
(Hebrews 12:1)

We can win every game if God be with us;
But it's impossible to win where there's jealousy and fuss.

We can win even though people put us down;
A team, which is determined, will never turn around.

We can win if we never worry whom the credit goes to;
It takes a team to win, not just me or just you.

We can win even though score-wise we're behind;
True winners are always winners by having love and peace of mind.

We can win if we neglect man and let God lead the way;
You see, man continues to change and we might be led astray.

We can win even when our fans turn us aside;
For we have that little something extra and that extra is our pride.

We can win on every opportunity if we'd all give our best;
Our team spirit and our pride won't let us settle for nothing less.

We can win if we'd all strive for the advancement of the team;
And at all times playing as one, giving in unto no other means.

We can win if we stop worrying about the hardships we go through;
Remember, God takes you under trouble water to cleanse and not drown you.

As I close with this poem telling you we can win;
Let's pray and work together believing that we can.

Inspired by God and written in reference to my high school basketball team

Written on: July 1, 1983

"AS A PLAYER"

"Know ye not that they which run in a race run all, but one receiveth the prize? So run, that ye may obtain." (1st Corinthians 9:24) "I can do all things through Christ who strengtheneth me"(Philippians 4:13)

As a player, I'm going to work hard
So I will always give my best;
And if my teammates fail to do so
I'll just be different from the rest.

As a player, I'm going to work hard
To make this team what it can be;
So, if it falls short down the line
I can remain self-conscious free.

As a player, I'm going to work hard
Giving my all until the end of the season;
So, if we never reach our goal;
No one will have a reason.

As a player, I'm going to work hard
Because our goal is to go to state;

I'm willing to do these things
But what about my other teammates?

Inspired by God and written in reference to my high school basketball team

Written on: July 7, 1983

"WHAT MORE DO YOU WANT?"

"But seek ye first the Kingdom of God, and His righteousness; and all these things shall be added unto you. Take therefore no thought for the morrow; for the morrow shall take thought for the things of itself. Sufficient unto the day is the evil thereof" (St. Matthew 6:33-34)

God gave His Son to die for our sins,
To show His love deep within.

He blesses us with food and clothes to wear,
He feels every pain of the burdens we bear.

He'll forgive us of our sins if we ask each day,
He's waiting on you to take time out to pray.

He gives us rain and sunshine too,
There's nothing too hard that God can't do.

He protects us with love and every arm of care,
He's a God that's never busy, expect Him everywhere.

He looks beyond our lives making sure the path is clear,
He's always on the lookout to warn us what's near.

Believe it or not, but one day you'll need this friend,
It's through Jesus only we have a chance to win.

Written on: August 10, 1983

"LOVE"

"Hatred stirreth up strife; but love covereth all sins" (Proverbs 10:12)

Love is the most powerful source on earth.

It's only a four-letter word, but its quantity and value stand great.

Love is something everyone desires, though everyone doesn't desire to love.

Why is this?

Isn't it written, "To have a friend thou must show thyself friendly?"

So it is with love.

I'd say, "To have love thou must show thyself loveable."

Another fact we can simplify is care. Everyone on earth wants to be cared for. The lonely, sad, rich, glad and even drunkards and prisoners. And so it is—love is care. To extend this fact a little farther, we can say that love is various things, which mostly cannot be said, but expressed.

Our expressions come from our actions. Our actions are our inner most feelings deep within which show how we feel about certain things. Whether our actions show good or bad, it's the way we feel, so therefore, we can say it's from the heart. Remember, what comes from the heart reaches the heart, whether bad or good.

There are many kinds of love. I'm not acquainted with them all, but I feel I know the most important one. The only love that will ever bring this whole world together and save us from destruction is Godly love. GOD IS LOVE.

Written on: August 12, 1983

"IF"

"If ye abide in me and my words abide in you; ye shall ask what ye will
and it shall be done unto you" (St. John 15:7)

If you can look up and see those things which are true;
And forget the bad things people say about you.

If you can put an end to all of your wrong;
And make a new start desiring to be strong.

If you can do the things that are constructive in your mind;
And when friends treat you wrong you still treat them kind.

If you can continue each day taking a step toward success;
And on every opportunity you always give your best.

If you can be wise and hold a level head;
When all sorts of things are being said.

If you can realize the things you want to do;
And never let gossip or trials hinder you.

If you can set some goals and have a desire;
To become that person you wanted as a child.

If you can be content and make the best of this life as you can;
I bid you farewell to that Promised Land.

Written on: August 12, 1983

"DEATH IS ONLY THE BEGINNING"

"For we know that if our earthly house of this tabernacle were dissolved, we have a building of God, an house not made with hands, eternal in the heavens" (2nd Corinthians 5:1)

Some say death is the end;
They fail to realize life just begins.
We'll never understand why our love ones pass;
Just keep your trust in Jesus and we'll make it at last.
God is at work taking His own up above;
He's concerned for us, but mainly it's His love.
When you see these things, take heed and be led;
Give up these earthly things, through Jesus let's be fed.
He promised He'd go to prepare a place for the upright;
He's making ready for us to view His Holy sights.
Be happy and go forth in God real strong;
He has blessed us truly, He'd never do us wrong.
Remember when He gave His Son for you and I;
That we might have a chance to choose the tree of life?

We serve a mighty God far beyond our mind;
And He's always near, using His own time.

Inspired by the terrible car accident that killed my dear friend and teammate, Shannon Rowland and her sister in November 1983

Written on: November 29, 1983

"WE'RE ALL GUILTY, HOW 'BOUT YOU?"

"For all have sinned, and come short of the glory of God" (Romans 3:23)

I've tarried upon this land for 17 years;
Day by day, I'm reminded of many tears.

Some tears to express the victory that God would bring;
Other tears to release the agony from doing wrong things.

Why study my life so closely neglecting to see the real you?
My faults you will find, why not admit yours too?

Is your life so complete you find time to bother others?
Or are you a part-time Christians keeping your devilment undercover?

God said, "Those things done in the dark would surely come to light;"
It's time you must realize that your wrongness will never be right.

I would seek unto God and unto Him would I commit my cause;
To live this life for Jesus is far greater than being lost.

Written on: January 1, 1984

"THE LAST FAREWELL"

"O death, where is thy sting? O grave, where is thy victory? The sting of death is sin; and the strength of sin is the law. But thanks be to God, which giveth us the victory through our Lord Jesus Christ" (1st Corinthians 15:55-57)

Oh! Jesus, it's been great to experience part of Thee;
The flowers, birds and sunshine have all become a part of me!

To awake each morning and hear the birds sing out;
Smelling the freshness of spring watching the flowers sprout!

A chance to live and grow bringing out the brightness within;
Revealing to all humanity it's Thee where true life begins!

Oh! It's great to be saved and sanctified washed freely from all sin;
I'm preparing day after day to hear Thy words, "come on in!"

I'm surely not afraid of any man nor am I about to doubt;
I've been watching, praying and believing too long I wouldn't dare change my route!

Written on: July 26, 1984

"THE POWER OF JEALOUSY"

"Jealousy is cruel as the grave: the coals thereof are coals of fire, which hath a most vehement flame"(Song of Solomon 8:6b) "For jealousy is the rage of a man." (Proverbs 6:34a)

Jealousy is man's greatest competition. It will cause hatred, fear, deceitfulness and many more unbecoming acts against God. The beauty of mankind, jobs, contests, games, politics and success are all areas in which jealousy exist. It is a conspiracy feeling one receive when he looks out in life and find something or someone who he feels is a bit more important than he.

Jealousy has caused man to fall short with God long ago, according to our Biblical stories. Satan, whom is the cause of jealousy, is the first victim and will be the last victim in which jealousy exist. His fear and uneasiness spirit that Adam and Eve would obey God cause him to tempt them in the Garden of Eden.

Then we see where Cain killed his brother Abel, because he allowed jealousy to control him. And so it was with Jacob against his brother Esau. Many Biblical stories reveal man's jealousy.

Jealousy will cause man to forget his Creator. It will even cause him to forget his roots and love ones. Jealousy will eat of man's flesh just as the dogs ate of Jezebel's soul. And once you allow jealousy a bite of your flesh then his desires become even greater for the remains.

Jealousy NEVER stops seeking! Oh, how foolish man will become! They become lovers of themselves and all earthly pleasures. Oh, how dim man's eyes get, slothful their minds become and betraying their hearts turn. When JEALOUSY rules!!

Written on: August 9, 1984

"MAKE ME WHOLE"

"Purge me with hyssop, and I shall be clean; wash me, and I shall be whiter than snow. Make me to hear joy and gladness; that the bones which thou hast broken may rejoice. Hide thy face from my sins, and blot out all mine iniquities. Create in me a clean heart, O God; and renew a right spirit within me." (Psalms 51:7-10)

Dear Lord, consider all my ways,
For against Thee I've truly sinned;
Create in me a clean heart, O God,
So I might magnify your love unto men.

I realize without Thee my life is futile,
No reason would I have to live;
Grant me that desire and determination,
So that my life unto you I will give.

Satan remains busy throughout the day,
Trying to turn my thoughts aside;
Lying, cheating and other sinful acts,
Unto these things He wants me to abide.

How long, Christ, will Thou keep away,
Thy Holy Spirit from my presence?

Guide me, direct me, with Thy power,
Help me to live in Thy grace forever.

Take this soul and renew its part,
Give it a bright light within;
Mold me and make me to Thy fullest,
That my soul may be set free from sin.

Written on: August 11, 1984

"A PRAYER FOR DELIVERANCE"

"In my distress I cried unto the Lord and he heard me. Deliver my soul, O Lord, from lying lips and from a deceitful tongue." (Psalms 120:1-2)

Dear God,

Don't let man continue to eat of my flesh. For they await my downfall and to hear the deepness of my cry. I must live for thee, for thou has bestowed many of thou beautiful works within me. They must be performed. God, don't let me grieve thou Holy Spirit for I long to please thee all of my life. Oh, Lord, it's thee and thee alone whom my heart desires to be full of. Though often times life's cavities sink within my mind. But Lord, I know you can and will cleanse a dirty heart and soul. Help me to defeat my foes; for surely the victory has already been won. Lord, you've planned, prepared and made a way, so all I ask is that you help me to keep your way and always keep it straight. Amen

Your Servant,

Written on: August 18, 1984

"TIME"

"To every thing there is a season and a time to every purpose under the heaven" (Ecclesiastes 3:1)

Time is one of God's greatest tools. Time is the key factor to our rising and fallings, preparation of food, sunrise and sunset, the awakening of the dawn of day, man's life and most of all the coming of our Savior Jesus Christ. Surely, time is in control. Not man nor his powers, but time itself is in control.

Have you ever stopped to observe this life? Just look around at men and all the earthly possessions they have stored up for themselves. They strive day after day building up an earthly kingdom. That's fine to strive in life, but they're striving for the wrong cause. Don't they realize God has already prepared a kingdom and time is the factor in which these things will be revealed? How long will men try to conquer time? Oh, foolish people, time will never be defeated for it is the solution to all of life's ways and plain life itself. Time is our ruler and governor.

A lot of people think time changes every so often, because we change constantly. I'm here to tell you that it isn't so. God, who rules and super rules the entire universe have placed time over the world. You see, God doesn't change His plans to meet our actions. If that were so, our God would be changing all through the day and every minute for our fickle ways. But you see, no matter which path we take nor whether we keep His laws, God's plan will always be unchangeable. God allows us so much time to do many things from day to day. But no, we think we have plenty of time, so we put off things until tomorrow. Don't you realize there is a set amount of time in each day that is given unto us so that we may do those things necessary for God? God is fulfilling His responsibilities. We are the shorter half.

I've so often heard men say, "There isn't enough time in a day to get done what's needed." Listen, oh blind men. God always provide for His cause. Why we put off so many things until tomorrow is simply because we spend a full day doing the wrong things. When I say wrong, I'm speaking of dwelling and seeking earthly things. But don't you ever think just because we spent a whole day wrong and misused God's time that He's going to continue to supply more given time. God is not going to wait on men. His covenant is certainly being fulfilled. It's we who must get in a hurry and catch time for time is proceeding daily according to our God. You can't control God or anything He puts out. God is on His way back to receive His own unto Himself and time is the final chapter.

THINK ON THESE THINGS: God is always with us so there is no reason for us to fall under Satan's snares. Trust God and let Him lead you through. Don't be deceived.

Written on: August 18, 1984

"IT'S TIME TO CLEAN UP"

"And ye shall hear of wars and rumors of wars: see that ye be not troubled; for all these things must come to pass, but the end is not yet. For nation shall rise against nation, and kingdom against kingdom; and these shall be famines, and pestilences, and earthquakes in divers places. All these are the beginning of sorrows" (St. Matthew 24:6-8)

Jesus is getting us ready. The time has come that all who are able to stand will stand and be lifted by the mighty love of God. Jesus has waited, been patient, and been elated to give us opportunity after opportunity to get His work done. Jesus is getting tired of idolatry, gay rights, open sin, and immorality. You'd better begin now and just now to pray and seek His face while He may yet be found. For the time is coming when no man thinketh on this hour Jesus will appear.

So many diseases have come about. They're finding all sorts of names for the diseases, but they can't find the cure. They're spending thousands of dollars trying to cure AIDS—a disease they never heard of. The doctors can't heal us. Medicine can't heal us. Jesus is getting tired of us living openly, unashamedly, and puffed up in pride against His Holy will.
Trouble is everywhere. People are talking about they just don't understand it. They claim people will do just any thing nowadays. Well…God is the same God as He was on yesterday and certainly these

are the same days of Noah. God doesn't change. These are the same days when Noah told the people it was going to rain.

And so it is, Jesus is on His way back. You'd better hurry and get your ticket signed and punched for Glory for He's near.

Church must begin in the home. Knowing the Lord is my shepherd and I shall not want, I must hold out until the end. If you're a Christian, you ought to act like it, walk like it, talk like it, and live that Christian life. It's time to clean up, people, for Jesus is coming real soon.

Written on: August 31, 1984

"WE GROW OLD"

"I have been young and now am old; yet have I not seen the righteous forsaken, nor his seed begging bread"(Psalms 37:25)

When we started in this life, nothing did we understand. As a child we listened, watched and became confused about people and their actions. Little did we fail to speak. We played and laughed, cried and made friends. No worries did we have. Life was a puzzle to us, but we never bothered to learn why. We continually kept in our small world and enjoyed those things around us. Then one day, we suddenly matured. It was then that we were made part of old folk conversations. Still little did we understand. All of a sudden, we encountered with a need for understanding. Still little did we have knowledge of. So, from there, we began to use our heads outside of just for a play box.

We became in need for wisdom and knowledge. Life was just beginning to work its cavities within us. Being our first problem, we had no knowledge of solving the problem, so we did what we thought was best. Later we found out our answer was the wrong one. It was then were we carried back to our childhood stage. Tears began all over even then. Being afraid to open up with anyone about our problems only caused fear and us more hurt.

Then we heard about a Savior; someone who gave His Son for our sins. Little still was understandable by us, but we gave it a try. We accepted Jesus as our Savior. Even then we continued to go deeper in trouble and sin. Thinking that accepting Jesus was enough was what carried us astray.

And as we matured more physically in life, the more sinful we became. Knowing Jesus was our Savior only made us more confused.

We couldn't understand why we were going through these things. We expected Jesus to keep us and protect us from all of our enemies and temptations. Then we later learned that we hadn't done enough to keep Jesus within. We had more or less driven Him away. So prayer became more vivid in our daily living. We understood somewhat better, but God brought us out. We began to really know God and not just "of" Him. He became the realest and the most sincere part of us.

Understanding, wisdom and knowledge were all available for the advancement of our walk with God. We found ourselves crying more than ever before; tears because of God's love, unsaved souls, our enemies and mainly for our very own sins. We realized God was a spirit. So, never again did we have to materialize back into this sinful generation. But from day to day we constantly repeat our mistakes. THINK: Why do we continuously grieve God? God brought us out long ago and no reason do we have for failure in this life.

Written on: September 1, 1984

"THINK ABOUT IT"

"Where was thou when I laid the foundations of the earth? declare, if thou
has understanding" (Job 38:4 and its entirety)

Have you ever stopped to think where the earth first began?
Some will tell you it was formed from matter, others will tell you by the
hands of man.

Did you ever stop to think how the moon, stars, and sun all came about?
Some will tell you by astronauts while others think they are from a
mysterious sprout.

Tell me, how is it that the planets all keep their balance and never collide
into one another;
Could it be some mighty manpower on earth? Or must we look much
farther?

Who causes it to rain and give the flowers and grains their growth?
Are they astronauts or men? Do you think it was both?

Written on: September 10, 1984

"IT'S COMING UP AGAIN"

"For we must all appear before the judgment seat of Christ; that every one may receive the things done in his body, according to that he hath done whether it be good or bad" (2nd Corinthians 5:10)

Lying, cheating, stealing and many other sins that we have committed throughout this life is coming around once again. No sin goes unpunished. We constantly sin every hour of the day; whether it's actually committing the sin in actions or just through an evil thought. We sin constantly. We are lying and killing one another over all these earthly goods, but God has much more to offer.

Written on: September 10, 1984

"THE POWER OF LOVE"

"And now abideth faith, hope, charity, these three; but the greatest of these is charity" (1st Corinthians 13:13)

Love is great and its powers are so unknown;
Love can offer you many friends, even though tomorrow they may be gone.

Yes, indeed love is a mystery that often grows but can't be seen.
Love gives today, take away tomorrow;
It dwells only in the pure and clean.

Truly, all of us love and are being loved by a mighty force from up above.

Written on: October 18, 1984

"BE THANKFUL"

"Rejoice in the Lord always; and again I say, Rejoice" (Philippians 4:4)

Be thankful always for God's gift of love.
Honor and cherish life for it is a gift from above.
Give out your all when there's more left to give.
Respect God and all His creations, in this way we must live.
Show a little love, humble yourself unto others.
Strive and grow upward working patiently together.
Give unto me what's mine and God will give you more.
Take time out for the sick and give encouragement to the poor.
Don't let this ole thing called life hurry and pass you by.
Don't you know by the time you learn how to live, it is then time to die?
Quit accepting life as it comes and giving the excuse that it was meant to
be.
Life has too much to offer us and those changes are up to you and me.
Don't constantly look at others trying to find fault in all they do.
I'm sure their life is already hell and they need not to catch hell from you.
Look up and live, believe beyond only the seen.
Remember, with out God you're just filthy rags and only He can make
you clean.

Written on: October 25, 1984

"YOU MAY GET BY, BUT YOU WON'T GET AWAY"

"Be not deceived; God is not mocked. Whatsoever a man soweth, that shall he also reap" (Galatians 6:7)

Men are trying anything just to see how much they can do;
Whether it's killing, robbing, or stealing, unto God these things are untrue.
Many have put God aside thinking now life path is sound;
It only takes God a second to bring you from higher ground.
Oh yes! It looks easy now and things seem to be going your way;
You just remember in this life every being will have his or her day.
The way seems to be hard and unrighteous unto the eyes of many;
God is immortal, yet so real, for you and me He offers plenty.
Go ahead, mock His name and grieve His Holy word;
But He's coming again oh so soon, yet a noise won't be heard.
Continue to love life and the pleasures it has to give;
You'd better realize at the same time, you're going to reap just what you live.
You just may get by now, but you won't get away;
He's going to return very soon, but there'll be no time to pray.

Written on: October 30, 1984

"I WANT TO BE FREE"

"Dearly beloved, I beseech you as strangers and pilgrims, abstain from fleshly lusts, which war against the soul" (1st Peter 2:11) If the Son therefore, shall make you free, ye shall be free indeed" (St. John 8:36)

Lord, I want to be set free from this world of sin;
No longer am I able to carry this load within.
I want to live and grow stronger each day by day;
Grant me your spirit so by your side I'll always stay.
I want to be free as the birds that sing in the air;
Mold me like the flowers that reveal your loving care.
Only if I could consistently seek thee and all that above;
Then I could say that I've truly taken a grasp of your love.
Oh, how free I'd like to be as the fish in the sea;
Having inner peace and radiant joy is my highest degree.
Lord, set me free as the wind so my life will touch many;
Give me a heart that's desiring and willing to help any.
I want to be so free that I'll shine brighter than the sun;
I want men to see the light that I've received from such a wonderful one.
If I could only be free like the waters so that my blessings would flow from within and without;
How great I'd feel to be free as the planets, radiating a fully-grown sprout.
God, please set me free like the rivers that flow;
Move in me mysteriously so the world may know.

I want to be free to say and do things I feel;
I want to keep an open mind and make my hopes real.
In you I know I can find that place for shelter and growth;
Help me to realize I must live for one, not you and man both.
I want to be free like the leaves on trees for they never have a worry;
Just to hang on to God's hand and reflect His beauty then my life I would not hurry.
Lord, I want to be free like Jesus was when He hung out on the cross;
Surely, physically He seemed to have been captured, but true believers know nothing had He lost.

Inspired by God as I struggled with accepting my calling to preach yet having been taught in a strict Missionary Baptist Church that women were not called to preach

Written on: November 16, 1984

"ENEMIES"

"Bless them which persecute you; bless and curse not. Recompense to no man evil for evil. Provide things honest in the sight of all men. If it be possible, as much as lieth in you, live peaceably with all men. Dearly beloved, avenge not yourselves, but rather give place unto wrath; for it is written, "Vengeance is mine; I will repay saith the Lord." (Romans 12:14, 17-19)

Love all of your enemies for this is right;
Embrace and respect them so in you they may see the light.

Pray for them today and once again tonight;
Learn to grow with them and teach them to walk upright.

What good is it to love only those who love you?
You need to experience with this spiritual force how to love those who have a different view.

Where will you find your strength and wisdom if you turn aside those unlike you?
How could you mistreat anyone then convince others you're true?

Enemies are your helpmates and from them you could receive plenty;
Remember, God has no respecter of people; what He does for you and me He'll do for any.

Written on: November 17, 1984

"A BROKEN VESSEL"

"Deliver me, O Lord, from the evil man; preserve me from the violent man" (Psalms 140:1)

Life is filled with uncertainties and disbeliefs;
Pains that are within are beckoning for relief.

We must learn as one together how to fight and not fall;
For soon it will be our day to answer the roll call.

Oh, it is so strange how rapidly we move for the sake of our own;
No time do we share with others and these people are left alone.

There are people who need our help just to carry their weight;
A kind word or listening ear could turn their entire life straight.

But this life we're living is so fastly live, we find no time for any others;
We should remember self-last, God first and secondly your brother.

One day we'll understand better why it's so important to give your best;
We'll understand why so many others were hurried and put to rest.

Written on: June 30, 1985

"PURPOSE FOR LIVING"

"For I know the thoughts that I think toward you, saith the Lord, thoughts of peace, and not of evil, to give you an expected end" (Jeremiah 29:11)

Why do we give ourselves so freely without any hesitation or fear?
Only to see our love and gratitude loss for someone who we felt was dear.

Many people give a little yet take a lot.
Never worrying about the next man for satisfaction they've already gotten.

So many are very negligence and stubborn, only out for their own good.
How must we stop these people and start teaching them the things we should?

We're living in a conditional time where words are seldom heard.
We must live and be a witness that there's reality in His Holy word.

We can't afford to take a step forward today then take two or three backwards tonight;
For we are living in an evil world and it's now that we must live right.

Written on: July 2, 1985

"I WON'T QUIT"

"We are troubled on every side, yet not distressed; we are perplexed, but not in despair; persecuted, but not forsaken; cast down, but not destroyed" (2nd Corinthians 4:8-9)

Even though today my life is filled with grief, tomorrow I will awake and search for relief.

My enemies are forever near awaiting to hear my cry, this gives me encouragement to live on and not die.

Trouble lies everywhere beyond my narrow way, I'm going to watch and seek, and then I'll bow to pray.

Seems like the farther I push upward the farther I'm moved back; this surely won't stop me because there's too much I still lack.

I won't ever stop reaching for what belongs to me in this life; I'm rest assured to be a winner if I endure through the pain and strife.

Sometimes I killed my own spirit trying to live like others do; yet I know where my hope lies and my faith too.

No matter how far I be shoved from my goal; I'm going to remain strong and strive to be made whole.

Maybe I'll never be what I desire nor reach my highest hope; but one thing I know for certain, I'll keep hanging on to the ropes.

Written on: July 2, 1985

"MYSTERIOUS LOVE"

"If ye were of the world, the world would love his own: but because ye are not of the world, but I have chosen you out of the world, therefore the world hateth you." (St. John 15: 19)

I have a prayer within my heart, it grows deeper day by day;
Broken promises and a loss of self-respect can be heard when I pray.

This prayer is one I never shared, because it carries great pain and fear;
A mysterious and untold love is why people draw so near.

Only if I could express to you and the world, these things barred within my soul;
Then you would clearly understand my lack of being made whole.

There is a well deep within, that no man has been able to reach;
It yearns for growth and wisdom, yet no teacher has been able to teach.

If only I could express to you and the world the pain and love I carry for all;
Many of you would flee from me and ignore the purpose for which I was called.

No man will ever understand this part of me, for it carries what none can bear;
It gives so kindly then take away, it reveals my burden and sincere care.

One day you will see me as I am and no more of what you believed;
Yet to understand where I am coming from, there's someone before me
you must receive.

Written on: July 2, 1985

"INDEPENDENCE DAY: ARE WE TRULY FREE?"

"The night is far spent, the day is at hand: let us therefore cast off the works of darkness, and let us put on the armor of light. Let us walk honestly, as in the day: not in rioting and drunkenness, not in strife and envying. But put ye on the Lord Jesus Christ, and make not provision for the flesh, to fulfill the lusts thereof"(Romans 13:12-14)

Why has everyone taken this day and treated it with a lack of care?
Exposing our selves in many fashions, out on the streets and everywhere.

This day is a celebration true, enough for it was when slavery was put to an end;
Oh foolish people, can't you see it was through Jesus we were able to win?

Then why have you abused this day showing no praises to Him above?
Having spent this entire day freely, you refused to express a little love.

We take life for granted and all that it is worth;
Human dignity and self-pride have abstained from the earth.

It's all right to shoot firecrackers and send many sparkles in the air;
Just remember it was Jesus who set us free, so why not show Him that we care?

Written on: July 4, 1985

"BLESSED CHILD"

"Ye have not chosen me, but I have chosen you and ordained you that ye should go and bring forth fruit, and that your fruit should remain; that whatsoever ye shall ask of the Father in my name, He may give it to you"(St. John 15:16)

Lord, never would I have thought unto so many I would give so much.
Even though sometimes I lack understanding, so many lives I continue to touch.

Many hear me with an open ear and unto constructive criticism they be led;
Yet many refuse to meet me on a daily basis, for they fear what might be said.

Thanks for using me so abundantly trusting me with thy Holy goods;
For I love sharing and giving with all of them throughout my neighborhood.

You have granted within my soul a forever giving love;
May I always use it effectively then return the praises up above.

Written on: July 16, 1985

"A SHADOWY GOODBYE"

"But as for me, my feet were almost gone; my steps had well nigh slipped"
(Psalms 73:2)

God, this is me again coming before you so poor;
I didn't plan for my life to be sailed on this lonely shore.
Sorry that it is so early and I'm writing a poem about the end;
Seems it's been so long ago since you and I were friends.
Everything was going just fine, at least that's what I thought;
Now your presence I have no longer and I see I've finally lost.
You've done what you could to give me a long and prosperous life;
Instead, I took advantage of it, now I'm filled with misery and strife.
My past seems to affect me even though it should not;
I find it hard to just let go and hold tight to what I got.
I've given up your pure and Holy Word to go live a dangerous way;
I know there's no hiding place for soon I'll have to pay.
So, this is just a thanks for what you've done for me;
I may never be able to repay you nor have the chance to become free.
When I've finally breathed my last breath and nothing else am I able to
do;
God, I want you to remember the times I gave myself to you.

Written on: February 7, 1986

"HE'LL CARRY YOU THROUGH"

"Then said Jesus unto his disciples, "If any man will come after me, let him deny himself and take up his cross and follow me. For whosoever will save his life shall lose it; and whosoever will lose his life for my sake shall find it" (St. Matthew 16:24-25)

When your way appears dark and no one seems to care; don't forget there's a God, take it to Him in prayer.

When your friends misunderstand and falsely accuse you; send your heartaches up above, for He knows just what to do.

When good lucks seems to fail you and bad luck takes control; this is no time for weakness, you must stand and be bold.

When mother and father have gone on high and you feel there is no way; remember Jesus cares so why not quietly bow to pray.

When the last mile of your journey has been put deeply in shame; look up and live for in heaven you have a new name.

Remember, men will always change for they're human like you and I; but there's One who is far greater than man and He lives far beyond the sky.

And to reach and get in contact with Him isn't very hard to do; just believe, confess and live the life and He'll surely carry you through.

Written on: February 12, 1986

"WE NEED ONE ANOTHER"

"Brethren, if a man be overtaken in a fault, ye which are spiritual restore such a one in the spirit of meekness; considering thyself, lest thou also be tempted. Bear ye one another's burdens, and so fulfill the law of Christ" (Galatians 6:1-2)

I wonder why sometimes we treat each other as we do.
Surely we know better, but I don't believe we want to.
I'm so tired of seeing us fall because we care less for the next man.
You see we're all in the same Army, marching in the same band.
Yet day-by-day we're constantly fighting among our very own.
By the time we come to ourselves, these people have passed and gone.
I'm tired of us using excuses saying, "That's the way it suppose to be."
If there was nothing we could do, then why did God make you and me?
We have become so lazy and stubborn, even deceiving our very own mind.
We're so wrapped up in material things that the Spirit you can't even find.
I'm tired of us sitting and waiting for someone to carry our weight.
If the rate of our actions were the key to Heaven, majority of us would be too late.
We're so blind and confused, daily destroying our fellowman.
Whether robbing, killing or giving them drugs this surely wasn't God's plan.
God made us to be helpers and helpmates one to the other.

We all have different task, yet we're still sisters and brothers.
Jesus came in the form of a man to symbolize what we must go through.
So, remember God takes you under trouble waters to cleanse and NOT drown you.

Written on: July 6, 1986

"WE NEED THE LORD"

"Behold, God is my salvation; I will trust and not be afraid; for the Lord
Jehovah is my strength and my son; He also is become my salvation"
(Isaiah 12:2)

Must Jesus bear this Cross alone and all the world go astray?
Must He continue to bless each of us daily and we go on living an
unrighteous way?

Must Jesus bless us with health and strength and we constantly complain
about how we feel?
Must He give us a soul and five good senses for us to do just as we will?

Must Jesus bless us with money, riches, houses, wealth and land?
Is it necessary that He keep watch on us as we pull from His helping
hand?

How cruel it is for us to live as we do knowing regardless He'll go our
bond.
As we go on battling one another He's revealing the victory has already
been won.

Christians, all we have to do is claim it!

Written by: August 8, 1986

"USE ME LORD"

"Also I heard the voice of the Lord saying, "Whom shall I send, and who will go for us? Then said I, Here am I; send me" (Isaiah 6:8)

If I can not do the will of God, then I would rather not exist at all.
You see, the will of God is a perfect place to be.
The will, a very special will, is good enough for me.

Use me dear Lord in any way you so desire;
Cleanse my soul and set it on fire.
Use me in the morning, at noon and at night;
For Satan will lose if I only attempt to fight;
Fighting all the evil and the darkness near my side;
I want Jesus to use me so that in Him I can abide.
Use me Lord, it doesn't matter when or where;
Only show me your will and safely lead me there.
Then I will open up my heart and let Jesus have His way;
So that I might touch many each and everyday.

Written on: April 27, 1987

"IN A CROWD, YET ALL ALONE"

"But Jesus said unto them, "A prophet is not without honor, but in his own country, and among his own kin, and in his own house." (St. Mark 6:4)

Have you ever been in a crowd having the best of times;
Setting your mind free as you left all else behind?

Giving and sharing with all without any hesitation or fear;
Including friends and strangers and to all whom you felt was dear.

Yet deep inside you felt alone even though a smile covered your face;
You then began to examine your self and wondered why you were in that place.

Then you got by yourself and you knew there was something left out;
Thinking back over the laughs you just had, something was still missing no doubt.

Know that God has a way of getting through to His people when we least expect His presence;
He gently approaches and speaks with a calm, still voice; if we're not careful we'll miss Him forever.

Written on: May 6, 1987

"I CRY"

"My God, my God, why hast thou forsaken me? Why are thou so far from helping me and from the words of my roaring?" (Psalms 22:1)

I hurt: I cry: I ache: I'm lonesome: I feel pain: I fear: I yet believe: I'm confused: I will wait: "The Lord is my shelter I shall not want" (Psalms 23:1): I give so freely: I'm rejected: I pray: I doubt: I yet believe: I will wait: I'm blind: I yet see clearly: "God is not mocked, whatsoever a man soweth, that also shall he reap" (Galatians 6:5): Suffering must come to all of us. No one can suffer for us. Jesus did already. I suffer yet I feel no pain: Jesus is near: He's watching over me just now: "Those who suffer need more than sympathy, they need companionship. I need: I want: I need Jesus: I want peace: I need love: I want companionship: I need patience: I want understanding: Tomorrow isn't promised: Today is all I have: I can't see the future: Is there one for me? Jesus knows: I constantly wait for tomorrow, but when tomorrow becomes today, I wished it were yesterday. History repeats itself: "To take up the cross is to give Christ service that costs time, money, work and tears." I'm carrying my cross: yet my light seems dim: I love the Lord: He's all I have: I will wait on Jesus: God is not through with me yet: Honesty is the best policy: "Take care of your life and the Lord will take care of your death" Jesus only requires for us to live Christ-like: giving, sharing, sowing, planting, confessing, strengthening, encouraging, magnifying, loving, believing, hoping, praying, trusting, taking, using, willing, and glorifying: Jesus is love: He's all I have: all I need: all I want: all I trust: God is magnificent: He's alive: breathing, watching, waiting, hoping, listening, sharing, and forgiving. He's all I need: God be with you and yours: He's mine: "A house is built by hands, but a home is built by hearts: Godliness and Love." The truth of a matter is not determined by how many people believe it.

When we live for the approval of God, we need not be disturbed by the opinions of others

Written on: May 8, 1987

"GOD'S CONSTANT LOVE"

"For love is strong as death" (Song of Solomon 8:6a)

Jesus has set me free from the danger of the earth;
I asked, sought, and knocked now I'm experiencing the new birth.
When trouble came my way, Jesus stood by my side;
He beckoned me to come, for in Him I could abide.
My thoughts became shattered, as my heart grieved with pain;
I consulted with old friends, still all seemed in vain.
I was falling short with God, as the days passed me by;
All because I lost faith with the One who lives up high.
Failing to realize each day that I'm nearing my own end;
Life was passing me by while I bowed my head in sin.
This isn't the way that God has planned for His very own;
We should be content always for our Father is on the throne.
So, to any of you whose discomfort and feel there is no way;
Remember, Jesus loves you so why not quietly bow to pray.
Regardless of your problem, God's a fixer of all things;
Just 'let go and let God' and watch the joy He will bring.
If you're sad, lonesome, and confused to the point of self-denial;
God is a just God; He'll give you a fair trial.
No matter what you've done nor how bad it may be;
Jesus is ready to forgive and truly set you free.

Satan is a liar as he tries to tell you there's no hope;
Believe me, God understands so hang on to your rope.
Because when I was down and I refused to seek God;
Jesus' forgiving love caused Him to chastise me with His rod;
I know the Lord will hear and answer our deepest desire;
For He has cleansed my soul and filled me with fire.
I thank God today and always for taking care of me;
He looked over all my faults and heard my honest plea.
Jesus loves us regardless though how stubborn we are to His will;
His love is a constant love no matter how we feel.

Written on: May 10, 1987

"MOTHERLY LOVE"

"Honor thy father and mother; which is the first commandment with promise" (Ephesians 6:2)

A true mother will take her child and give him to the Lord;
Trusting in Jesus alone to keep her child on one accord.

A true mother will pray daily, in the morning, noon and night;
Casting her cares upon the Lord to bring her child upright.

A true mother will bring peace in the church and out on the streets;
Knowing that love must start at home, she lets Jesus guide her feet.

A true mother will bring her children joy and her husband the highest respect;
Giving and sharing with all mankind, many lives she constantly affect.

A true mother will sit and listen to a stranger as if he was her very own;
Realizing Jesus loves us all and none does He want to feel all-alone.

A true mother is humble and sensitive to the needs of all others;
And these such qualities of a woman well spoken has been given her the name "Mother."

Written on: May 10, 1987

"HE'S WORTHY TO BE PRAISED!!!"

"Bless the Lord, O my soul; and all that is within me, bless his holy name"
(Psalms 103:1)

Oh, Jesus I can't express the joy you've given me;
My soul is on fire now that I'm set free!

Free to go and do, and truly speak from my heart;
Telling the whole world in Jesus I found a new start!

I'll tell it everywhere each and every day;
How Jesus snatched me from sin when I had gone astray!

Oh yes, Jesus deserves the very finest and our complete best;
Because He's given us His all that we might find rest!

The birds sing His praises, the flowers reveal His loving touch;
The green forest shouts, "He's Alive!" and to all He has given so much!

Truly, Jesus lives and He's worthy to be praised;
For He is my all and all forever and always!

Written on: May 12, 1987

"MY SAVIOR'S WANTS & MY SAVIOR'S NEED"

"But ye shall receive power after that the Holy Ghost is come upon you: and ye shall be witnesses unto me both in Jerusalem and in all Judea, and in Samaria and unto the uttermost part of the earth." (Acts 1:8)

I want to be more like Jesus in my heart. Jesus has blessed us so and I'm shame to say, but I've failed to give Him the honorable thanks that He deserves. All that He has made is good. Nothing is misplaced, out of order, in the way or disposable in the Lord's sight. Where we have fallen short with God is that we've taken everything, which is good and misused them…we're simply out of His will. Jesus wants us to be happy, successful and prosperous human beings lacking nothing. Yet we shortage ourselves by trying to obtain the seen and unseen using the wrong motives.

Jesus is a fair and just God. He has already told us that He would put no more on us than we can bear. Some think it's impossible to please God; of course not. If that was so, then Jesus wouldn't be the fair and just God He claims to be. Why would He ask us to obey Him? Obeying Him is not something beyond our strength or reach, for He has written His word within our hearts and placed the truth upon our lips. Remember, Jesus has ALL powers. Satan's power was broken when Jesus got up out of the grave. Honesty and confession of our sins should be our aim daily with the Lord. You see, Jesus is coming soon. There is no time for doubting, disbelief, falsehood or for sin period. If you really know the Lord, ask for His mercy and forgiveness just now.

I'm so thankful and happy, yet shame and aching. You see, Jesus loves us. He's constantly giving us the things we need and He's trying to embrace and understand our every want. Have you ever stopped to think just how much we constantly want from day to day? Imagine us not receiving these wants. Quickly, we become frustrated with ourselves, others and mainly God. Also, have you ever stopped to think just how many things we constantly need from day to day? But we never put much emphasis on our needs for we know that God lets it rain on the just as well as the unjust. Realize it or not, everyone needs are taken care of daily at times when we're not conscious of what we're in need of. God will supply our every need.

Now wait a minute. Have you ever stopped to consider Jesus' wants and needs? Listen to such a broken voice crying in the wilderness. Jesus is a jealous God. He hurts too when His wants and needs aren't fulfilled. Now you might wonder just what does Jesus want and need? Well…Jesus wants every lost sheep to be found and He needs every found sheep to be productive and prosperous. You see, it hurts Jesus when He calls out to sinners wanting them to stop, listen and receive Him as their very own. Jesus cries and weeps over His lost sheep. Then Jesus hurts even more when those found sheep get too busy to stop, listen and be obedient to His will. Jesus needs all of His found sheep to respond to His calling. Whether preaching, teaching, giving, sharing, listening, weeping, loving, glorifying or magnifying, we all form one body. Therefore, it is very necessary that 'EVERY SAVED SOUL SEEK THE SINNER'S SOUL, THEN SOON ALL SOULS WILL BE SAVED.' Remember, Jesus has wants and needs too and we are the answers to fulfilling His wants and needs.

Written on: May 22, 1987

"WILL YOU BE READY?"

"And many of them that sleep in the dust of the earth shall awake, some to everlasting life and some to shame and everlasting contempt" (Daniel 12:2)

There's going to come a time in life when we all must bow at the feet of Jesus. For God said, "Every knee shall bow and every tongue shall confess that Jesus Christ is Lord." He's coming at the hour that no man thinketh He shall appear. Many wonder what they will be doing when Jesus returns. The most important issue on that day will be if we're prepared to meet the Lord. Truly, if our hearts are right then our place of dwelling will be of the right spirit also. Whether we are on the mountain or whether we are down in the valley, we do know God is there. He has promised to never leave nor forsake us.

Oh, many are out in their own world foolishly chasing after the wind; failing to realize that they have got to die one day. Yet Christ said, "Many people are already dead." You see, this death He is speaking of is spiritual death. And this death is the most dangerous and deadly of them all. Understand, if we are spiritually dead then there is no after life for us. Therefore, we must experience death twice. First, here in this life and secondly, on Judgment Day.

Many fear not the Lord and His commandments. Walking, many times running after the cares of this world. Don't they realize these things are only temporary? God asked the question, "What profits a man to gain the whole world and lose his only soul? It's simply grasping for the wind.

Christians must always be ready for the enemy. Mind you, Satan appears to us through many objects, situations and people of this world. (Many times through our very own love ones) Yet we shall not fear. But why are we so afraid? Why do we become so weak? We are living in the last days and there is not time for weakness, lack of faith or giving up. God is our strength, our fortress in the time of trouble. Whom shall we fear? Surely we have mountains to climb and seas to swim, but the victory is already our. We must proclaim it. So, why fear? Knowing the race is not given to the swift nor to the strong, but to he that endureth until the end, why not just hold out? Hold out, regardless of the circumstances you're encountering at the present. For God is going to return real soon.

Written on: June 3, 1988

"A TRUE SOLDIER"

"Put on the whole armor of God, that ye may be able to stand against the
wiles of the devil" (Ephesians 6:11)

This love that we carry deep within our souls;
Is an expression of Jesus' love and our desire to be whole.

You have shown me so much care and unspeakable love;
God understands our cry as He receives our prayers up above.

I'm glad to know that you and I are as close as we are today;
I know we have true love, because we've both given some away.

You're not the same person that I met a few days ago;
You have accepted my true calling and not once have you said no.

Thanks for giving me what you have and all that it is worth;
There has been a great change, even a spiritual birth.

Truly, you are Heaven-sent for your heart is constantly seeking growth;
Remember, you can only live for one, not God and man both.

With Jesus you will always find that strength and understanding you seek
so dear;
Just 'let go and let God' because He'll always be near.

Oh, don't forget about ole Satan, because he surely hasn't forgotten about you;
He's anxiously plotting your next fall trying to capture your spiritual view.

But you are of a different breed, not a failure, indeed a strong man;
To fall and to not get up is to fail, yet you now stand.

So, be careful and always aware of the pits Satan prepares for you;
Study, pray and watch, then Jesus will safely lead you through.

Don't ever give in because there are still so many trials we must overcome;
Be patient, yet eager to go and finally we'll reach home.

You are 'A True Soldier" equipped for all of life's aches and pains;
Hold out until He comes for you, bringing the reward you are living to gain.

Written on: August 27, 1988

"BE STRONG, DON'T GIVE IN"

"Though He slay me yet will I trust in Him" (Job 13:15a) "But He knoweth the way that I take; when He has tried me, I shall come forth as gold" (Job 23:10)

Is your life full of trouble and your heart grieved with pain?
Does confusion clog your mind wondering what the next day might bring?

Are you happy, full and complete with yourself as well as all others?
Does contentment rule your desires as you mingle with your sisters and brothers?

The way gets rocky and weary as we climb toward new heights.
Though it gets dark and gloomy at times, we must maintain our spiritual sight.

Are you afraid, lonely or confused about your true position in life?
Then I challenge you to remain at ease as you face heartaches and strife.

For it is written that disappointments shall come to all who reverence the Lord.
Though attacked on every side, we must remain on one accord.

But for those of you who look not to God, but unto your own strengths.
Be wise, go search for Him today, because His Son, for your sins was sent.

Acknowledge your weakness and failures for confession is a must.
Allow God to have first place in your life and there you can build your
trust.

And if you trust Him for one thing then learn to trust Him for all.
For He has never lost a case nor missed a telephone call.

Go and be strong as you face the new day giving God all that you can give.
Because life is too short and death is too sure for you to die having not yet
lived.

Written on: October 6, 1988

"BE FREE BUT COMMITTED"

"What shall we say then? Shall we continue in sin, that grace may abound?
God forbid. How shall we, that are dead to sin live any longer therein?"
(Romans 6:1-2) "For to be carnally minded is death; but to be spiritually
minded is life and peace" (Romans 8:6)

As you go you're way discovering new ground;
Keep Jesus in mind remembering in Him you are found.

Be open to suggestion from others as you consider your own;
Learn to follow as you lead, soon you'll be led home.

Your works goes unspoken among many of your friends;
Yet your award awaits you in Heaven, it's not a gift from man.

God has set you free to live as you so choose;
Be smart, give each day back to Him or else you will lose.

I understand many times that things don't go your way;
Being a God-fearing man, you know the price we must pay.

Times have been hard and who knows, they may get worse;
Giving God what He deserves, bring blessings and not curses.

So learn the ways of God and His will for you;
Be determined, dedicated and committed in all that you do.

Written on: August 12, 1989

"COMING HOME"

"The Lord is nigh unto them that are of a broken heart; and saveth such as be of a contrite spirit. Many are the afflictions of the righteous; but the Lord delivereth him out of them all." (Psalms 34:18-19)

Who are you?

What is your name?

What race are you?

What is your game?

Where were you born? Just who are your parents? Do they make you feel loved?

…Yes, I hear your love as you speak to me real loud.

Yet I wonder why you holler as if you're speaking to a crowd.

I can't help but wonder sometimes if you really, really care.

Because I seem to rattle your emotions making life uneasy to bear.

I just want to be loved by you and to know that my life is worth living.

Inspired by a television movie I watched in Canberra, Australia: "I Know My First Name is Stephen"

Written on: August 23, 1990

"KEEP ME IN YOUR LOVE"

"Search me, O God, and know my heart; try me, and know my thoughts.
And see if there be any wicked way in me, and lead me in the way
everlasting" (Psalms 139:23-24)

Dear God, I stand before you acknowledging all of my sins,
I've failed to live by the spirit and move when He said when.

Just to stop and look back on yesterday and the days before;
I can see you were always there giving me a reason to live for.

Yet I was very self-centered and anxious to be my own guide;
To live for anyone else, I felt my wants would be denied.

As time went on I begin to doubt if I would ever become free;
Though I wasn't locked behind bars, I was a prisoner at another degree.

Time taught me to overcome all of my fears or else they would overcome
me;
Your love taught me how to break down the barriers so that I might
clearly see.

Now to see me as I truly am and no more what I protest to be;
I really wonder why you chose to first love me.

As I read your Holy word and ponder on your mighty love;
I say, "Thank you for everything" for I know all good things come down
from above.

Inspired by God and written while I lived in Canberra, Australia. I was in the "Land Down Under" playing professional basketball and working for the Australian Government. Sounds like life was great, right? No, far from it! I was like Jonah, "boarding the first ship" (in my case, plane) trying to flee from God's calling on my life to preach the gospel of Jesus Christ. He finally won.

Written on: April 25, 1990

"MOVE BY THE SPIRIT"

"Not by might, nor by power, but by my spirit saith the Lord of hosts"
(Zechariah 4:6b)

God has been good to us all, just look around and see;
Shelter, food and clothes have been provided for you and me.

Let's get in the spirit, live for God whilst we may;
We must put aside excess weight as we face another day.

After giving His life on the Cross, is this too much to ask?
Knowing the pain Jesus suffered, living for Him we should make our task.

I'm bothered by this world and all the destruction that's within;
How everyone is on a rampage, living carelessly without the thought of
sin.

It's easy to be deceived and miss the path that is planned for you;
For Satan will catch you off guard aiming to capture your spiritual view.

Yet we must remain free so that we're conscious all the way;
So, when trouble seems to be near, all we have to do is pray.

Stay alert and watchful for your decisions should be made with care;
Because you're laying down sound virtues in your home and everywhere.

Written on: June 12, 1990

"YOU ARE THE EAGLE IN OUR MIDST"

"Even the youths shall faint and be weary and the young men shall utterly fall: But they that wait upon the Lord shall renew there strength; they shall mount up with wings as eagles; they shall run and not be weary; and they shall walk and not faint." (Isaiah 40:30-31)

The eagle has long broad wings and she's very strong with soaring flight;
She holds the highest rank amongst her class, as she possesses keen eyesight.

She chooses a mate and by him she stands for the remainder of her life;
She finds honor and respect in being a devoted wife.

She clings to her flock making sure they're safe and sound;
She goes through extreme measures to plant each on a solid ground.

Yes, you are that eagle that I've described just now;
You possess all of her characteristics and many more, and I'll tell you how.

You travel up and down the road many times alone;
Your course set before you, your heart so strong.

You run to our rescue during the day and all through the night;
You pour out your love and embrace us giving us the strength we need to
fight.

Fighting whatever is set before us, you hold us hand in hand;
You remind us that Jesus cares and in Him we must stand.

We admire your courageous spirit and determination to do God's will;
We stand in awe in your presence as you declare that He is real.

Many find your words tough for sometimes they cut deep;
Even the holiest saint reevaluates his life and weeps.

Many take heed to your words and promise to live better on tomorrow;
Yet many won't let you in and they remained filled with sorrow.

Some are watching and waiting to see what befalls you;
Maybe not hoping the worse, but just to see what you'll do.

Some wish they had the power you possess, but are not willing to bear that
cross;
They marvel and may discredit your efforts, desiring to be like you, but be
their own boss.

Yet we know that Jesus rules your life for this you make clear;
He's the one you live and work diligently for each year after year.

You often steal from your mind and give where we lack;
Understanding the strength you give is added strength we give back.

By your words, our faith increases through trial with error;
Eliminating all fear of any worldly terror.

Truly, you are that eagle soaring in our midst each day;
As you protect us with your wings of love, we know we're blessed in a very special way.

Inspired by God and written to my dear pastor, Rev. Endia J. Scruggs on her 7th year anniversary as pastor.

Written on: January 5, 1996

"GOD'S RESTORATION POWER!"

"Come unto me all ye that labor and are heavy laden and I will give you rest. Take my yoke upon you, and learn of me; for I am meek and lowly in heart; and ye shall find rest unto your souls. For my yoke is easy and my burden is light" (St. Matthew 11:28-30)

God is able to lift the most weakest and burdensome soul;
He's the only one who can heal and make each of us whole.

When you are down in the valley and life's pressures are piercing your heart;
Go to Jesus in prayer and pick up the pieces making a new start.

Only when you are low beyond seeing the stars shining real bright;
God's strength emerges from deep within causing you to become a light.

So, know that trouble will surely come, but it can't last always;
It's just a cleansing and refining mechanism helping us to turn from our wicked ways.

And once you are refined and begin to walk according to His will;
Old man trouble is going to come knocking again in attempts to make you doubt that which you know is real.

Yet God warns us of present and future danger when we study His Holy
Word;
He speaks softly as Satan yells loudly, if you're not careful you'll wonder
whom you've heard.

God is waiting on you to call on Him and speak what's on your mind;
He may not come when you want Him but He's sure to be on time.

Confess your sins to Him and hold out until the end;
Resist the devil as you go and finally you will win.

Written on: April 4, 1997

"TROUBLE"

"Man that is born of a woman is of few days and full of trouble" (Job 14:1)

Trouble has a way of perplexing one's inner spirit causing one to refocus. Trouble comes to us all regardless of our race, age, religion, beliefs, titles/ positions, riches, poverty, and our moral beliefs. It will cause one to reach deep within and find out what one is truly made of. Trouble has a way of making man to stand still and face himself—pricking and testing man's heart to the degree that either man will cry out to God in mental anguish or perhaps give in to Satan through alcohol, drugs, sex, and many other unbecoming acts against God. Trouble comes just like a thief in the night. Yet those whom belong to God, he warns them of present and future danger. One still is never prepared nor ready to greet trouble. It comes all through the day. You can't hide from it. It is sure to find each and every one of us. Trouble comes and attacks us through all areas of our lives.

Just when you think you have discovered the key to success, the road to happiness, or the way to live, old man trouble hits and staggers you helping you to know nothing is secure in this world. You work hard all of your life to buy a fine home, car, and other material assets. Then a tornado, earthquake, flood, or fire comes overnight destroying all of your possessions. Insurance or not, no one ever wants to see destruction take everything that it took many years to acquire. You go to college or perhaps not, yet you manage to land a good job with good pay, excellent benefits, and what appears to be a rewarding future. You work many years and receive one or maybe many promotions, waiting the day you will retire. Overnight you are told the company is closing, moving overseas or perhaps just closing for good. Even if they assist you in getting another job, the many years of hard work have now been all lost. When trouble comes. You find a wife or husband and plan to spend the rest of your lives together as you build your family. Then Satan attacks the home for he knows God wants to use families to carry out His will. Then and only then does it become easier for Satan to get that husband, wife, and those children once he conquers and divide. When trouble is on the rise.

However, Jesus tells us to rejoice and be glad when trouble comes for it is only a test of our faith. We are told to be not overcome with evil, but to overcome evil by doing good. Dr. King said, "Only when it is dark enough can men see the stars." My brother and sisters know that trouble will come knocking and sometimes crushing down your door. But know that it is your friend. If we would only learn how to take all of our troubles and allow them to have there way for the moment—truly it is only a moment when you know the award that awaits you then we would not develop ulcers, headaches, stress, and attitudes with God nor the perpetrator. For we wrestle not against flesh and blood. (Ephesians 6:12) Yet we are more than conquerors through Christ Jesus our Savior and Redeemer. Know that trouble is our mighty helper. For it teaches us how to trust in God, wait on God, and how to rest in God. When it hits my brothers and sisters, having girded ourselves with the whole armor of God, ride old man trouble out. It will surely subside. Trouble doesn't last always. Yet if we would only seek first the Kingdom of God and His righteousness, trouble would never knock us off course. It would only confirm that we are children of God and walking in His way. Trouble is coming to us all. So, make sure your suffering is for the Lord's sake and not for Satan. St. Matthew 10:16—Jesus tells us "Behold, I send you forth as sheep in the midst of wolves; be ye therefore wise as serpents and harmless as doves." In the same chapter and in verses 34-37, it tells us that Jesus came not to bring peace to the earth, but a sword. He tells us that our worse enemies will be in our own home. Also, He tells us that if we can't forsake father, mother, son, or daughter before Him then we are not worthy of being His. Forget not, God is a jealous God. So, once you have matured in the Lord, you will know that trouble does not spell tragedy for God's people, however, trouble does spells triumph. Go and be strong in the Lord. Just learn to wait on the Lord. Isaiah 40: 29-31 tells us "He giveth power to the faint, and to them that have no might he increaseth strength. Even the youths shall faint and be weary and the young men shall utterly fall. But they that wait upon the Lord shall renew their strength; they shall mount up with wings as eagles; they shall run, and not be weary; and they shall walk and not faint." Learn to embrace each and every trouble that comes your way for it has many blessings in store for you. Trouble is our friend. It's Gods blessing in disguise.

Written on: April 19, 1997

"WHO CAN BE COMPARED TO HIM?"

"For our God is a consuming fire" (Hebrews 12:29)

Oh God, who are we to question your will and your perfect way?
Both life and death is in your hands, mere man can't take them away.

You speak in the thunder that roars, through the flower that's smiling in
the rain;
The mountains reveal your great majesty, out on a hill you endured our
pain.

In the valley you designed your personal faith lab, in which all men is
surely to past through;
Having past and failed many tests along the way, our walk with you is
made anew.

Power is released when you speak Lord, and things move at your mighty
command;
We are challenged to gird ourselves and fight like warriors, having done all
to stand, we stand.

Not as weak vessels on yesterday, but a people determined to endure until the end;
We have put on the whole armor of God, prepared to fight Satan and his friends.

Don't leave us through the night oh Lord, as we rest upon our beds;
And when we awake on tomorrow we will seek you, knowing following you we won't be misled.

Written on: April 26, 1997

"YIELDED, NOW I'M FREE"

"For though I preach the gospel, I have nothing to glory of; for necessity is laid upon me; yea, woe is unto me, if I preach not the gospel. For if I do this thing willingly, I have a reward: but if against my will, a dispensation of the gospel is committed unto me" (1st Corinthians 9:16-17)

When I was a little girl, I wanted the Lord to save me;
He said, "My grace is sufficient for all so come unto me."

At 8 years old I accepted Him as my Savior and was determined to do His will;
Self was in need of crucifixion because for Christ I wanted to live.

Denying self day by day hasn't been easy for me to do;
The Spirit and flesh are constantly at war, I'm in need of constant rescue.

But as I have grown in the Lord and studied His Holy Bible;
I have a closer walk with Him and I've learned life is about survival.

Doesn't matter if I get wounded nor experience pain along the way;
I know God is who He says He is so I must continue to pray.

I don't have to be first nor the strongest to enter God's place;
Neither do I have to be the swiftest just as long as I finish <u>my</u> race.

God must be first in everything and I must learn to wait;
Just because I can't see Him moving doesn't mean that He's late.

I have learned through many pains and suffering that God wants every part of me;
Self-service and trying to please others kept me from being free.

Yet I can tell you now that I'm free and I thank God for His love;
My desires are to please Him in all of my ways and then return the praises above.

Oh, it's good to be saved and sanctified and washed freely from all sins;
I await the day I can hear my Lord say, "My child thou has entered in!"

Inspired by God and written when I accepted my calling to preach on June 8, 1997

Written on: July 11, 1997

"GIVING THANKS"

"In everything give thanks; for this is the will of God in Christ Jesus concerning you" (1st Thessalonians 5:18)

Every day is truly a day of Thanksgiving. As we gather together and enjoy good food and our families, we should be reminded of all that God has done for us. Thanksgiving broken down gives you thanks/giving. Therefore, we need to give thanks unto God who has done all the giving. He teaches us how to give thanks as read His Word. The book of Psalms is filled with thanks and praises unto our God. Also, Ephesians 5:20 tells us not to give thanks when all your bills are paid, when there's enough food on the table, when your relationships are without problems, when there's peace in your home, church, or community, when you have a stable job, nor when you can handle your own business. The scripture simply tells us to "give thanks always for all things…" That's pretty self-explanatory, to the point, and covers all areas.

We have no excuse for doing anything other than thanking our God. It doesn't matter that things are not going your way. Paul assures us in Romans 8:28 that all things are working for our good and best interest if we are true believers and followers of Christ. We need to learn how to thank God when everything, and I do mean absolutely every possible thing, has gone wrong in our lives. This really is where the blessings are. From my own personal experiences, I've come to discover 3 very significant things relevant to getting what you want from God and they are as follows: 1) We must seek God's counsel first and find out what His will is for our lives. Our problem is that we already have our lives mapped out and chosen the way we're going to live it. "Seeking Him first is our only reasonable service." 2) Even though the Bible is filled with God's promises, we never reap many of them, because of our disobedience. Once we find out what it is God would have for us to do, we must be willing to follow. We need to learn how to follow as we lead. (Follow God as we lead others unto Him) We simply want to live any kind of way and yet expect God to keep His Word. Yes, He does, but only to those who obey Him. Obedience is the key. 3) God is not going to do for us what He has enabled us to do for ourselves. I don't care how much we beg and plead with Him. There are too many handicap Christians. Taking some initiative on our part is crucial to reaping the promises of God.

Lastly, Philippians 4:7 tells us to "Be careful for nothing; but in everything by prayer and supplication, with thanksgiving, let your request be made known unto God." So, the scripture is telling us that we should tell God what we want or need, but with the attitude of thanksgiving. God expects for us to call upon Him, but to come with a joyous heart. We need to take our minds off of our situations and focus on God alone. Know that God already knows what you need and perhaps want, but He's looking for someone with the right mindset and attitude. Rejoice in the Lord! Again, I say rejoice! As we make preparations for Thanksgiving, let us not forget the real reason we are to be thankful. If it wasn't for God's longsuffering and mercy unto us, many of us would not be able to gather for family dinners, because our disobedience would have destroyed us. Yet God's hand of mercy is ever present, keeping us from the enemy. Rejoice and be glad!!!

Written on: October 21, 1997

"A DECEITFUL, DESPERATE & WICKED HEART"

Jeremiah 17:9 says, "The heart is deceitful above all things and desperately wicked; who can know it?"

Proverbs 16:25 says, "There is a way that seems right to a man, but the end thereof leads to death."

1st Peter 5:8 says, "Be sober, be vigilant; because your adversary, the devil, walking about as a roaring lion, seeking whom he may devour."

Jeremiah says that the heart is deceitful above all things and desperately wicked…The heart that Jeremiah is talking about is not the heart that's located in the left wall of our chest that pumps blood throughout our body. No, the heart he's referring to is the mind, the thoughts, and the desires of mankind. He says that the heart is deceitful…deceit, as we know is to be tricky, to be dishonest, to lie, to know the truth but intentionally present or portray something opposite of the truth. To scheme, to show trickery, to have ulterior motives, even wrong motives. Deceit is to simply satisfy one self. It is to hide or cheat or steal. Simply, being a "friendly enemy." Jeremiah says man's heart is full of deceit. So full of it that it's crookedness is or outweighs everything else about that individual. In other words, man's own desires, when left to himself, without God, without the Holy Spirit being an influential part of his life; he will self-destruct. Man's heart is so crooked and desire to do bad things that this is greater than any other evil. He goes on to say and "desperately wicked." Have you ever been desperate for anything? If so, then you can relate with this word desperate within this context of scripture. When one is desperate s/he will go to extreme, most of the times, foolish measures to obtain what it is that s/he wants. Examples are: a drug, crack, and cocaine addict will steal and even sell his or her body for drugs; a student will risk cheating and getting caught on an exam when he knows he hasn't properly studied and prepared himself; a mother, when her babies are hungry, cold, and dirty will work two, three and four jobs to make ends meet; a lover will give up his or her body if they fear losing their mate to another. One who's desperate for money will rob you, or me even while we are at home asleep as well as banks. A mother or father who has a sick child will get up all times of the night and rush that child to the Emergency Room to save that child's life. Talking about being desperate.

Desperate versus Addiction: There's good and bad with and in them both. And we know that when one is desperate, he is anxious, uneasy, not stable, jittery, and somewhat nervous. So, Jeremiah is saying that our hearts anxiously wanting to do wrong; that we are very evil. Then 1St Peter 5:8 says we need to stay sober and vigilant (alert and watchful) because the devil is seeking someone to devour (eat up greedily). If man's heart is already full of deceitfulness and wickedness, then the devil is also seeking us out; it almost seems as though we can't be any other thing but bad. We can't go any other way but down. No, but thank God, He knows man's heart. In Psalms 139, David tells us that God knows our thoughts from afar off and that before we even get words off of our tongues, He knows them completely. Jeremiah asked the question, "Who can know it?"

Well…the next verse tells us that God examines our hearts. Proverbs tells us that a man think or believes he's heading in the right direction, but the end of it—his thoughts, decisions, and actions lead to death. We must be very prayerful as well as careful on the road that we are traveling. I surely don't want to <u>assume </u>that I'm traveling the right path and be lost in the long run. Sure. Many ways "seem" right but one does not truly know if s/he is traveling the straight and narrow path until s/he seek God's counsel and get in His will. Therefore, people of God, we need God! We need Him to take hold of our hands no doubt. But moreover, we need Him to take control of our minds and thoughts, because if we are not careful, we all are subject to self-destruct. That's why we must do as David did in Psalms 51. We must repent, confess, and cry out to God that against Him we have sinned. Not only should we confess our sins daily, but also we must ask sincerely for God to "Create in me a clean heart oh God, and renew the right spirit within me." (Psalms 51:10) We must be willing to allow God to do a daily spiritual checkup on our hearts.

Written on: October 21, 2003

"THE ROADS OF LIFE"

"Enter ye in at the straight gate; for wide is the gate and broad is the way, that leadeth to destruction, and many there be which go in thereat" (St. Matthew 7:13)

There are many roads in life that we have a choice of following. Typically, they boil down to two roads. Good and evil. We want the best out of life. We like to wear the best clothes, the best shoes, and the best jewelry; we want to drive the finest cars, live in plush houses, and dine at the finest of restaurants. We want the best, easiest and highest paying jobs. And we many times seek pleasure in all sorts of sporting events, theme parks, hobbies, and each other trying to satisfy our flesh. However, what we many times fail to realize is that typically where there are a lot of people and a lot of self-seeking pleasure and glorification, God is NOT present (including some churches). We let crowds and numbers deceive us into thinking that God is in the majority and therefore we MUST be traveling the right road.

For example, there are two roads I can take from my house to get to Old Railroad Bed. God may often tell me to take the long road. It's not as popular; it's not fun every step of the way; neither is it the shortest way. But it is the <u>best</u> way to travel if God tells me to take this road. Another way may be shorter, less hills, less potholes in the road, etc. But God knows the best way for me to travel and what is needed for me on this "road of life."

However, on the other hand, the shortest way is the way the devil usually encourages us to travel. It's full of adventure, excitement, friendly enemies, and fun! The devil wants us to take this road as he pricks and poke at us telling us the lie that the road is "shorter and we need to hurry, hurry, hurry and it will get us to Old Railroad Bed faster. The first trick of his is to convince you that he desires to get you to Old Railroad Bed. Don't be deceived. He simply desires for you to do it, do it, do it until you're satisfied, whatever it is! His desire is to kill each and every one of God's people according to St. John 10:10a which says, "The thief cometh not but for to steal, kill and destroy."

Know that God desires for you and to I have a good life and the best things out of life according to St. John 10:10b "…but I have come that ye might have life and have it more abundantly." Yet God desires to give us blessings in intervals so that we can get to know Him. But the devil desires to give us everything today, right now, instantaneously causing us to use the wrong tactics to get the material stuff, but he doesn't show us the end result. The end results are jail time, prison time, pregnancy, sexually transmitted diseases, loss of joy and peace, a spirit of depression, rejection, anger, hatred, bitterness, isolation and incredible, non-ending debt. Finally, we will find ourselves walking in guilt, shackles and shame. For the Word of God says "that to be carnally minded is death, but to be spiritually minded is both life and peace."

Written on: October 26, 2003

"FIGHT ON!"

"For we wrestle not against flesh and blood, but against principalities, against powers, against the rulers of the darkness of this world, against spiritual wickedness in high places" (Ephesians 6:12)

You are a courageous soldier whose endured many battle scars;
Your sword and shield you keep close by, as you enter every war.

Oh, your weapons are truly not carnal, nor made by man's hand;
For you have been 'fashioned for His glory' as you work the Master's plan.

Many scars are a direct hit from being put on the front line;
Your wounds came from many 'secret agents' as you've taken blows of mine.

Yet you stand front and center, ain't afraid of no enemy's camp;
Squared shoulders, head high, feet planted, God's word you take as a lamp.

To guide you into every dark place even into the minds of so many;
You preach and teach with power that will shake the foundation of any.

Some come running and falling down confession they need a Savior;
Others frown and roll their eyes refusing to submit to their Creator.

Yet you have not altered His word nor compromised for the sake of a few;
God says, "Pastor Scruggs, keep doing what you're doing and one day
He's going to welcome you!"

*Inspired by God and Written to my dear Pastor, Rev. Endia J. Scruggs
when her mother passed away on February 2, 2006*

Written on: February 5, 2006

EPILOGUE

I pray that the Spirit of the Living God has ministered unto your mind, soul and spirit as you read this book of poems and writings. Know that "God is that Spirit" for 2nd Corinthians 2:17 tells us "Now the Lord is that Spirit: and where the Spirit of the Lord is, there is liberty." God desires for us to be free, walking in the true liberty that His Son, Jesus, came and gave His life for. Because of the life, death, and resurrection of Jesus, you and I no longer have to be bound by sin, our past, our guilt, our failures, nor our mistakes. We can walk in the true liberty that God has called us to. For Galatians 5:1 tells us to "Stand fast therefore in the liberty wherewith Christ hath made us free and be not entangled again with the yoke of bondage." Many of God's people have been made free by accepting Jesus as their Savior, but by the snares of the enemy, have found themselves "entangled again" with sin.

True freedom comes from recognizing who God, His Son Jesus and His Holy Spirit really are; learning their attributes and then realizing who we are in them. We truly are heirs for Galatians 3:29 tells us "And if ye be Christ's, then are ye Abraham's seed, and heirs according to the promise." We must understand that what was promised to Abraham in Genesis 13:14-17 is the same promise that belongs to us. For it says, "And the Lord said unto Abram, after that Lot was separated from him, Lift up now thine eyes, and look from the place where thou art northward, and southward, and eastward and westward: For all the land which thou seest, to thee will I give it, and to thy seed for ever. And I will make thy seed as the dust of the earth so that if a man can number the dust of the earth, then shall thy seed also be numbered. Arise, walk through the land in the length of it and in the breadth of it; for I will give it unto thee." Yet to receive the promise, we must believe it and know that it applies to us today and then go boldly to God in prayer to petition Him for the promise. However, the utmost principle that must be applied to obtain the promise is OBEDIENCE. We must walk in obedience to receive all that God has for us. We must obey God even when He calls us to "tough places" and to do "tough things." Obedience is the key to unlocking every promise of God.

I thank God for my cousin Denotee Martin who lives in New Albany, MS for allowing God to speak through him to me last June 2005 during the tragic death and loss of his brother. Denotee simply told me "There are people's destinies that are connected to me. And until I "fully" get in my place, those people can not become all they're supposed to become, because I'm not in my place. He told me that some people's destinies will be lost, aborted, and never reached all because I never "fully" got in my place." I want you to know, I felt so convicted by the Spirit of the Living God by your words that I began to <u>step out of fear</u> and <u>step into greater boldness</u> determined that I WILL allow God to birth and bring out of me all that He has put in me so that no one, connected to me, will lose their way. Well…this book is one of the many tools that God showed me I must do to "fully" get in my place. The ministry God birthed through me, "Taking It By Force Outreach Ministries Inc." is another tool that God revealed unto me that was needed in order that I "fully" get in my place. I finally realize it's not about what I want but what God has birthed in me from the beginning according to Jeremiah 1.

ABOUT THE AUTHOR

Rev. Dr. Valerie Martin-Stewart was born in Water Valley, MS to the late Hervie and Louise Martin-Pope. She has one special daughter named Paris Marie. A special aunt and uncle named Aunt Annie and Uncle Joe Martin who lives in Taylor, MS, raised her since she was 8 years old. Valerie is currently employed with the U.S. Army as a civilian Electrical Engineer in Huntsville, AL.

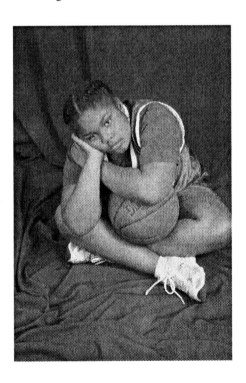

978-0-595-39376-3
0-595-39376-4

Printed in the United States
51364LVS00006B/1-225

9 780595 393763